W9-ASR-108

$12|14$

Hickory Flat Public Library
2740 East Cherokee Drive
Canton, Georgia 30115

Beans to Chocolate

by Lisa M. Herrington

Content Consultant
Dr. Rich Hartel, Professor of Food Science, University of Wisconsin

Reading Consultant
Jeanne Clidas, Ph.D.

Children's Press®
An Imprint of Scholastic Inc.
New York Toronto London Auckland Sydney
Mexico City New Delhi Hong Kong
Danbury, Connecticut

Library of Congress Cataloging-in-Publication Data
Herrington, Lisa M.
  Beans to chocolate/by Lisa M. Herrington.
    p. cm. — (Rookie read-about science)
  Audience: 003-006.
  ISBN 978-0-531-24741-9 (library binding) — ISBN 978-0-531-24707-5 (pbk.)
1. Chocolate—Juvenile literature. 2. Cacao—Juvenile literature. 3. Chocolate
processing—Juvenile literature. 4. Cocoa processing--Juvenile literature. I. Title. II.
Series: Rookie read-about science.

  TP640.H47 2013
  664.5—dc23   2012035028

Produced by Spooky Cheetah Press

Photographs © 2013: age fotostock: 24, 30 bottom, 31 center top (Giovanni
Mereghetti), 27 (Yoko Aziz); Alamy Images: cover top center, 16, 30 center top, 31
bottom, 31 center (Bon Appetit), 28 (IS2 from Image Source); AP Images/Sipa: 19,
20, 30 center bottom; Corbis Images/Richard T. Nowitz: 15; Getty Images: cover
top right, 23, 30 second from bottom (James L. Stanfield/National Geographic),
4 (White Packert/The Image Bank); Shutterstock, Inc.: 3 top left (Graham Taylor
Photography), 3 bottom (Vlasov Volodymyr), cover bottom (Yuliyan Velchev);
Superstock, Inc.: cover top left, 7, 31 center bottom (age fotostock), 3 top right
(Flowerphotos), 11, 12, 30 second from top, 30 top, 31 top (imagebroker.net), 8
(Science Faction).

Table of Contents

Candy from Trees!

Do you like chocolate? Many people do! Let's learn how it is made.

Chocolate can be made into many types of treats, like candy.

Chocolate comes from cacao (ka-KOW) trees. The trees are found in warm, wet places. They grow big fruit called **pods**.

Cacao pods grow straight out of a tree's trunk and branches.

pods

8

It is hard to imagine these seeds as a chocolate bar!

Inside the pods are seeds. Those are the **cacao beans**. They give chocolate its taste.

Cacao pods grow to the size of footballs. About 20 to 50 seeds grow inside each pod.

Drying the Beans

Farmers cut the pods from the trees. They remove the beans.

A worker spreads the beans out to dry in the sun.

The beans are put under banana leaves to bring out their flavor. They stay there for about a week. Then the beans are dried in the sun.

FUN FACT!

Long ago, people used cacao beans as money. For example, a horse could be bought with 10 beans.

At the Factory

The hard, dried beans are placed in large bags. They are sent to factories all over the world.

> Factory workers unload bags of cacao beans from a train.

The beans are **roasted** in ovens. That brings out more of the flavor.

The beans are stirred as they roast.

Next, a machine takes the shells from the beans. The soft insides are called **nibs**.

The nibs are the only part of the beans that are used to make chocolate.

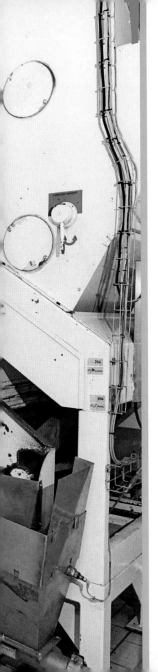

A machine grinds the nibs. They will become liquid chocolate.

A worker puts the nibs into the machine.

Mix and Mold

The liquid can be mixed with milk and sugar. That is how chocolate candy is made.

The ingredients used in milk chocolate are measured carefully before mixing.

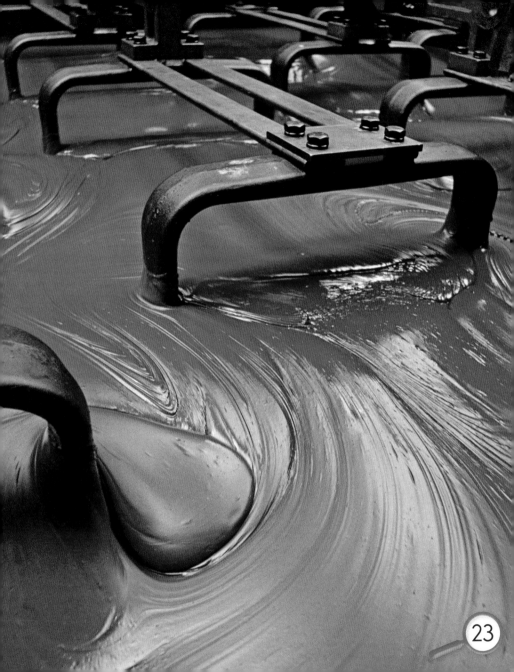

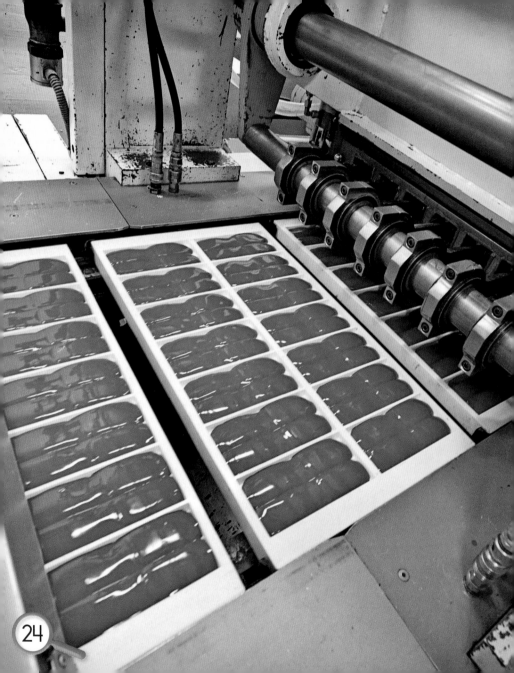

The mixture is poured into candy **molds**, such as bars.

This machine is filling candy bar molds.

The chocolate cools.
It becomes hard.

Chocolate can
be molded into
many shapes.

Chocolate bars can be made from milk chocolate (like the candy this girl is holding), dark chocolate, or white chocolate.

At last, the chocolate is ready to eat. Yum!

FUN FACT!

Americans eat about 12 pounds of chocolate per person each year.

Making Chocolate
Step by Step

 **1.** Cacao beans are taken from trees.

 **2.** The beans are dried and sent to factories.

 **3.** The beans are roasted in ovens.

 **4.** The shells are removed. The nibs are ground into liquid chocolate.

 **5.** The liquid can be mixed with milk and sugar.

 **6.** The mixture is poured into molds.

Glossary

cacao beans (ka-KOW beens): the seeds of the cacao tree used to make chocolate

molds (mohlds): hollow containers that liquid can be poured into so that it sets in that shape

nibs (nibs): the soft insides of the cacao bean after roasting

pods (pods): fruit that holds seeds

roasted (roh-sted): cooked in an oven

Index

Facts for Now

Visit this Scholastic Web site for more information on how chocolate is made:
www.factsfornow.scholastic.com
Enter the keyword **Chocolate**

About the Author

Lisa M. Herrington writes books and magazine articles for kids. She lives in Trumbull, Connecticut, with her husband and daughter. She has a sweet tooth for chocolate!